ONE
YEAR
WISER

A GRATITUDE JOURNAL

Mike Medaglia

SELF
MADE
HERO

First published 2016
by SelfMadeHero
139-141 Pancras Road
London NW1 1UN
www.selfmadehero.com

Written and illustrated by Mike Medaglia

Publishing Director: Emma Hayley
Publishing Assistant: Guillaume Rater
Sales & Marketing Manager: Sam Humphrey
UK Publicist: Paul Smith
US Publicist: Maya Bradford
Designer: Txabi Jones
With thanks to: Dan Lockwood

A CIP record for this book is available from the British Library

ISBN: 978-1-910593-21-9

10 9 8 7 6 5 4 3 2 1

Printed and bound in Slovenia

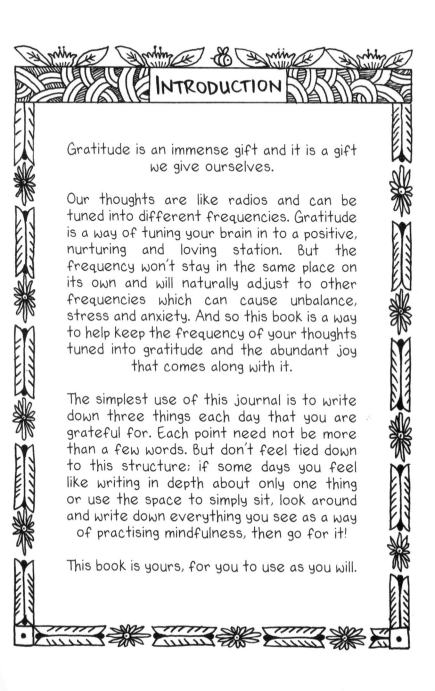

INTRODUCTION

Gratitude is an immense gift and it is a gift we give ourselves.

Our thoughts are like radios and can be tuned into different frequencies. Gratitude is a way of tuning your brain in to a positive, nurturing and loving station. But the frequency won't stay in the same place on its own and will naturally adjust to other frequencies which can cause unbalance, stress and anxiety. And so this book is a way to help keep the frequency of your thoughts tuned into gratitude and the abundant joy that comes along with it.

The simplest use of this journal is to write down three things each day that you are grateful for. Each point need not be more than a few words. But don't feel tied down to this structure; if some days you feel like writing in depth about only one thing or use the space to simply sit, look around and write down everything you see as a way of practising mindfulness, then go for it!

This book is yours, for you to use as you will.

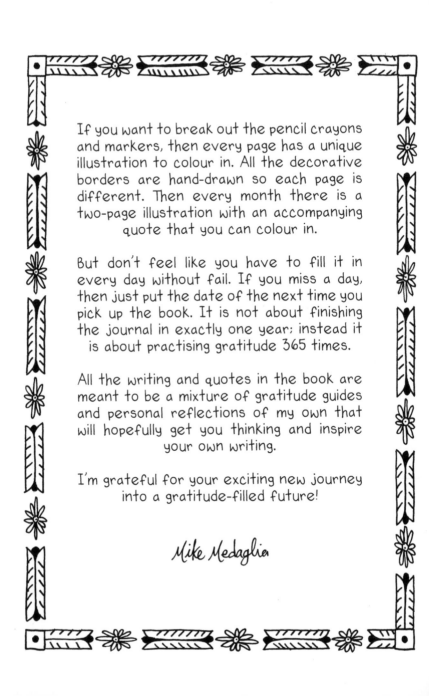

If you want to break out the pencil crayons and markers, then every page has a unique illustration to colour in. All the decorative borders are hand-drawn so each page is different. Then every month there is a two-page illustration with an accompanying quote that you can colour in.

But don't feel like you have to fill it in every day without fail. If you miss a day, then just put the date of the next time you pick up the book. It is not about finishing the journal in exactly one year; instead it is about practising gratitude 365 times.

All the writing and quotes in the book are meant to be a mixture of gratitude guides and personal reflections of my own that will hopefully get you thinking and inspire your own writing.

I'm grateful for your exciting new journey into a gratitude-filled future!

Mike Medaglia

FIRST ENTRY

Below is the space for your first journal entry. Use it as a time to think gratefully about your plans and dreams. Think about the excitement and motivation they give you. Consider how they enrich your life. Also, this is a time to remember that both small and great adventures begin with a first step.

DATE:

_____

_____

_____

_____

_____

_____

_____

DATE: 5/1/19.

I am grateful for:
- My beautiful children. Healthy
        smart, funny!
- Harley, my baby girl
- Jeff. kind heart, sweet soul
- Our beautiful home that keeps us safe.
- Having all that we need and want

DATE:

DATE:

WAKE AT DAWN WITH A WINGED HEART AND GIVE THANKS

DATE:

FOR ANOTHER DAY OF LOVING. ~ KAHLIL GIBRAN

DATE:

DATE:

DATE:

If there is a new project or hobby you have been wanting to learn or improve upon, set yourself some manageable goals to get the ball rolling. In a sense, you can lower your expectations for yourself. Set aside some time for your pursuit and then choose to accomplish half of what you think you could get done in that time period. The lack of pressure makes the work more fun and meeting your goals brings satisfaction!

IF YOU WANT TO BE FREE,

GET TO KNOW YOUR REAL SELF.

LINJI

DATE:

DATE:

DATE:

DATE:

DATE:

DATE:

DATE:

Give in to all your generous impulses.
If you think there is something kind you
can do for another creature, then do it.
Acting on kindness is self-fulfilling because
the reward is in the action.

DATE:

DATE:

DATE:

LIFE BEGINS AT THE END OF YOUR COMFORT ZONE.

DATE:

NEALE DONALD WALSCH

DATE:

DATE:

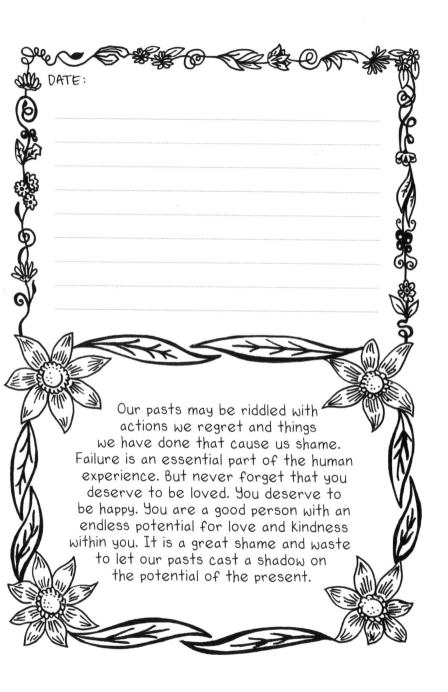

DATE:

Our pasts may be riddled with actions we regret and things we have done that cause us shame. Failure is an essential part of the human experience. But never forget that you deserve to be loved. You deserve to be happy. You are a good person with an endless potential for love and kindness within you. It is a great shame and waste to let our pasts cast a shadow on the potential of the present.

DATE:

DATE:

DATE:

DATE:

I DON'T THINK OF THE PAST. THE ONLY THING THAT MATTERS IS THE EVERLASTING PRESENT. ~ W. SOMERSET MAUGHAM

DATE:

DATE:

DATE:

Routine is a great way to give
our lives structure and balance
while allowing us to accomplish a lot
in a day. However, there have been times
when I feel my routine means that I stop
noticing the passing of a day as I go from one
task to another. A wonderful remedy for this
is to do something different. I will occasionally
walk a different route on my daily commute
or go to an event that I normally wouldn't
make time for. Experiencing new things
is a way of acknowledging the limited
time we have to experience the
endless variety in life.

NOTHING IS A WASTE OF TIME IF YOU

DATE:

DATE:

USE THE EXPERIENCE WISELY. ~ RODIN ~

DATE:

DATE:

DATE:

DATE:

DATE:

I find the chaos of a dense forest so comforting. Nothing has been arranged with any thought or overall plan. Yet everything, every mossy rock and fallen tree, feels like it is exactly where it should be. Everything looks so natural in natural spaces. The way to encourage the same natural feeling in ourselves is to act as nature does and let things fall, and grow, where they will.

DATE:

DATE:

DATE:

DATE:

DATE:

DATE:

DATE:

I'm so grateful for you. Your existence. And this brief time we get to connect through this book. Thank you for you.

DATE:

I'M CHASING MY DREAMS STRAIGHT TO THE TOP

DATE:

DATE:

INTO A SKY THAT HAS NO LIMITS. ~ ROBERT M. HENSEL

DATE:

DATE:

DATE:

DATE:

Take a moment to
acknowledge something
that causes you anxiety. Going
forward, when you find yourself
thinking about this thing, use
that as a reminder to stop,
breathe and be mindful of your
surroundings. Turn unwelcome
anxiety into a positive and
balancing activity.

DATE:

_____

_____

_____

_____

_____

_____

_____

_____

TAKING TIME TO DO NOTHING OFTEN BRINGS

DATE:

_____

_____

_____

_____

_____

_____

_____

_____

_____

EVERYTHING INTO PERSPECTIVE. ~ DOE ZANTAMATA

DATE:

DATE:

DATE:

_____
_____
_____
_____
_____
_____
_____
_____

DATE:

_____
_____
_____
_____
_____
_____
_____
_____

DATE:

Look down at your hands.
Try to think about all the
things you do with your hands
on a daily basis. All the things you
achieve with them. Your hands are
a lesson in gratitude that you have
with you constantly. In moments of
doubt, look at your hands and remind
yourself of all you can do with your
eight fingers and two thumbs.

DATE:

THERE IS NOTHING EITHER GOOD OR BAD,

DATE:

DATE:

BUT THINKING MAKES IT SO. ~ WILLIAM SHAKESPEARE

DATE:

DATE:

DATE:

DATE:

Although there are always
unanswered questions in life, it
can be beneficial to sit and ask the
universe new questions. There is no
need to guide the questions; instead
let the questions rise out your own
heart. They will not only offer new
paths to focus on, but can be used
as a map to understand better
where our hearts want to go.

DATE:

LONELINESS AND THE FEELING OF BEING UNWANTED

DATE:

DATE:

IS THE MOST TERRIBLE POVERTY. ~ MOTHER TERESA

DATE:

DATE:

DATE:

DATE:

I love watching birds soar on the wind. They normally have to work hard, flapping their wings, in order to fly forward. But when they catch the wind, they go with it and ride it out, covering great distances in a shorter period of time. There is a wisdom in this, in taking opportunities when they present themselves and utilising those opportunities to help move us forward.

DATE:

DATE:

LAZINESS MAY APPEAR ATTRACTIVE,
BUT WORK GIVES SATISFACTION.

ANNE
FRANK

DATE:

DATE:

DATE:

DATE:

DATE:

Build your day around your
spiritual practice, be that prayer,
mindfulness or meditation. If you try
to squeeze your spiritual practice
into your day, it can feel like a
chore and often get ignored. Give it
the prominence in your life that it
deserves and all the rest of your
time will feel the benefit.

IT IS NOT JOY THAT MAKES US GRATEFUL.

DATE:

DATE:

IT IS GRATITUDE THAT MAKES US JOYFUL. DAVID STEINDL-RAST

DATE:

DATE:

DATE:

DATE:

DATE:

Some of the richest
experiences of life result from
our own personal inner journeys. The
experiences of inner growth can't be bought
or traded and have no fiscal value, so it is
common not to make time to explore them.
But by missing them, we are missing so much
of the magic this life offers up. It is like
having a fresh, crystal clear lake beside your
house, but not taking the time to dip your
feet in or go for a swim. Make some
time to test the waters of your soul
and explore the hidden treasures
deep within you.

L I

IS
SO BEAUTIFUL
THAT DEATH HAS FALLEN
IN LOVE WITH IT, A
JEALOUS, POSSESSIVE LOVE
THAT GRABS AT
WHAT IT CAN.

BUT

LIFE
LEAPS
OVER OBLIVION
LIGHTLY, LOSING ONLY
A THING OR TWO OF NO
IMPORTANCE, AND GLOOM
IS BUT THE PASSING
SHADOW OF A
CLOUD...

YANN
MARTEL

DATE:

THE SEARCH FOR COURAGE IS ONE

DATE:

DATE:

OF LIFE'S GREAT ADVENTURES. ~ MAYA ANGELOU

DATE:

DATE:

DATE:

DATE:

Try to end the day with thoughts of gratitude. When laying in bed, after all your chores and demands have been dealt with (or can wait until the morning), take a moment to reflect and be thankful for:

- Your bed, pillow and sheets, and the comfort they give you.

- The rest your mind and body can get over the course of the night.

- All the other people benefiting from the darkness to rest their minds and bodies.

Open the door to gratitude before sailing off to sleep and travel through your dreams on the thoughts it brings in.

DATE:

FEAR MAKES STRANGERS OF PEOPLE

DATE:

DATE:

WHO SHOULD BE FRIENDS. ~ SHIRLEY MacLAINE

DATE:

DATE:

DATE:

DATE:

_____

_____

_____

_____

_____

_____

_____

Be creative. It is a way of saying thank you
to the world. Nature gives us so much beauty
to observe and interact with. We can return
the favour by using our talent (whatever
that may be) to create more beauty for this
world and the creatures in it.

DATE:

HE WHO KNOWS THAT ENOUGH IS ENOUGH

DATE:

DATE:

WILL ALWAYS HAVE ENOUGH. ~LAO TZU

DATE:

DATE:

DATE:

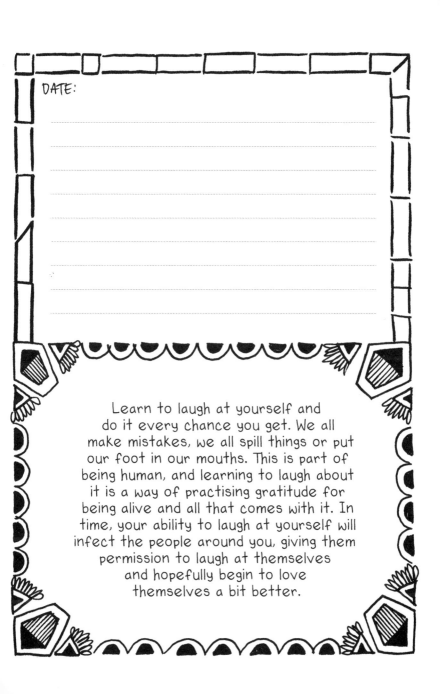

DATE:

Learn to laugh at yourself and
do it every chance you get. We all
make mistakes, we all spill things or put
our foot in our mouths. This is part of
being human, and learning to laugh about
it is a way of practising gratitude for
being alive and all that comes with it. In
time, your ability to laugh at yourself will
infect the people around you, giving them
permission to laugh at themselves
and hopefully begin to love
themselves a bit better.

WHEN YOU ARE GRATEFUL, FEAR DISAPPEARS

DATE:

DATE:

AND ABUNDANCE APPEARS. ~ TONY ROBBINS

DATE:

DATE:

DATE:

DATE:

DATE:

Often, experiencing the
opposite of one thing will remind
us of how wonderful that thing is.
If we always eat rich-tasting food, then
eating simply seasoned and cooked foods
can taste refreshing and nourishing
in comparison. It works the same with
gratitude: if we live our lives taking all
the abundance we have for granted,
then taking time to be thankful for
the riches in our lives will fill us
with waves of gratefulness
and satisfaction.

NOBODY CAN GO BACK AND START A NEW BEGINNING,

DATE:

DATE:

BUT ANYONE CAN START TODAY

DATE:

AND MAKE A NEW ENDING.

~ MARIA ROBINSON ~

DATE:

DATE:

DATE:

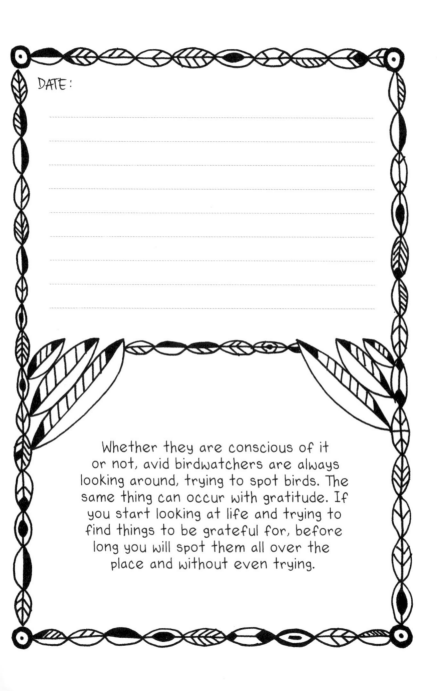

DATE:

Whether they are conscious of it
or not, avid birdwatchers are always
looking around, trying to spot birds. The
same thing can occur with gratitude. If
you start looking at life and trying to
find things to be grateful for, before
long you will spot them all over the
place and without even trying.

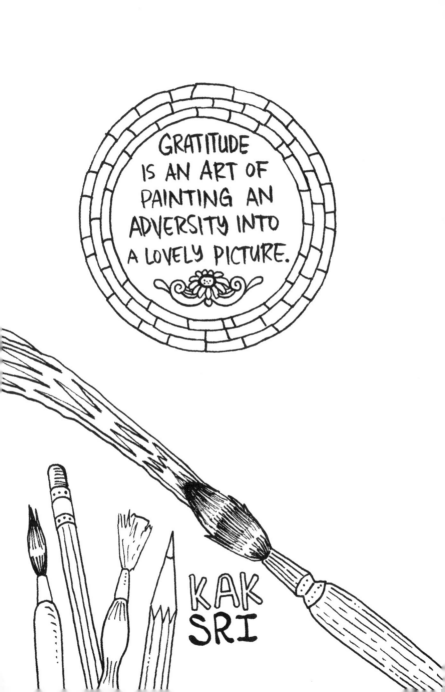

DATE:

LET GRATITUDE BE THE PILLOW UPON WHICH

DATE:

DATE:

YOU KNEEL TO SAY YOUR NIGHTLY PRAYER. ~ MAYA ANGELOU

DATE:

DATE:

DATE:

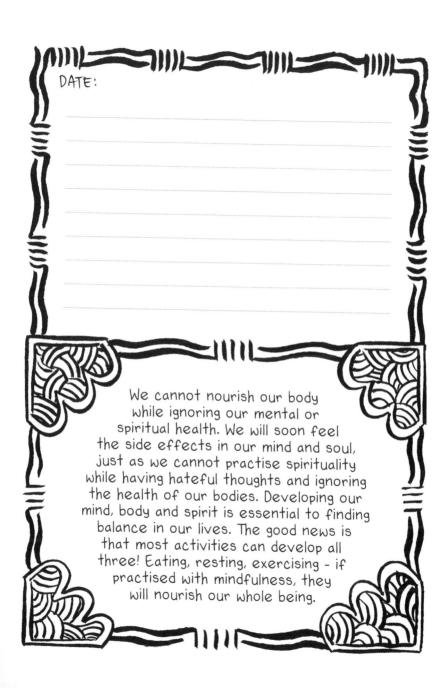

DATE:

We cannot nourish our body
while ignoring our mental or
spiritual health. We will soon feel
the side effects in our mind and soul,
just as we cannot practise spirituality
while having hateful thoughts and ignoring
the health of our bodies. Developing our
mind, body and spirit is essential to finding
balance in our lives. The good news is
that most activities can develop all
three! Eating, resting, exercising - if
practised with mindfulness, they
will nourish our whole being.

DATE:

ALWAYS DO WHAT YOU ARE AFRAID TO DO.

DATE:

DATE:

RALPH WALDO EMERSON

DATE:

DATE:

DATE:

DATE:

Sometimes, when I go on a hike and am surrounded by the beauty of the natural world, I catch myself thinking about work or tensions I am experiencing with other people. When I notice myself doing this and am able to bring my mind back to the present, my thoughts no longer run in circles but instead are focused on the wonder of this moment. Over time, I have come to realise that if I stop at any moment and look around me there is always something amazing to focus on that I might easily have missed if I had stayed caught up in my thoughts and myself.

DATE:

DATE:

DATE:

DATE:

DATE:

DATE:

DATE:

Take a moment to listen to your heartbeat.
Imagine the amazing journey your blood takes
through your body, moved along by the beating
of your heart. This journey happens over
100,000 times each day. If we can acknowledge
the importance of each beat, then we can
carry gratitude with us constantly.

DATE:

DATE:

THE CONSCIENCE LIKE INDIVIDUAL RESPONSIBILITY. ~ ELIZABETH CADY STANTON

DATE:

DATE:

DATE:

DATE:

DATE:

Over the coming days,
try to acknowledge
these things in nature:

• Birdsong.

• Interesting tree bark.

• Spaces where nature and the
human world come together, like weeds
in the cracks of cement.

Nature is an endless source
of beauty and inspiration, but
occasionally we may need
to remind ourselves to take
a second and enjoy it.

GRATITUDE UNLOCKS THE FULLNESS OF LIFE. IT TURNS WHAT WE HAVE INTO ENOUGH, AND MORE. IT TURNS DENIAL INTO ACCEPTANCE,

CHAOS TO ORDER, CONFUSION TO CLARITY.

IT CAN TURN A MEAL INTO A FEAST, A HOUSE INTO A HOME, A STRANGER INTO A FRIEND. GRATITUDE MAKES SENSE OF OUR PAST, BRINGS PEACE FOR TODAY AND CREATES A VISION FOR TOMORROW.

MELODY BEATTIE

DATE:

THOUGHTS ARE ENERGY. AND YOU CAN MAKE YOUR WORLD

DATE:

DATE:

OR BREAK YOUR WORLD BY THINKING. ~ SUSAN L. TAYLOR

DATE:

DATE!

DATE:

DATE:

Eating is a perfect time to practise
mindfulness and gratitude. When we sit
to eat, we can reflect on how the food we
are eating was grown, processed and transferred.
The food didn't just appear in the grocery store
for you to buy. Also, eating is one of the most
essential but also pleasurable parts of being alive,
so it should be easy to look down at your plate
and be thankful for the food on it. If you do
struggle to be grateful, then simply try to picture
the plate empty with you having no way of filling
it with food. Not everyone in this world has
an abundance of food and you are
immensely lucky if you do.

DATE:

DATE:

DATE:

DATE:

LIVING WITHOUT AN AIM IS LIKE SAILING WITHOUT A COMPASS. ~ JOHN RUSKIN

DATE:

DATE:

DATE:

If there is a person in
your life who is upsetting
you, take some time to imagine
what it is about them that is causing
them to act in the way that you find
upsetting. We are all suffering internally; it
is a part of being human. By learning to be
compassionate towards the suffering of
people who cause us suffering, our ability
to be compassionate evolves, allowing us to
extend loving kindness to everyone we
come into contact with. At the very
least, you may be able to make a
friend out of an enemy.

THE PURPOSE OF OUR LIVES IS TO BE HAPPY. ~ DALAI LAMA XIV

DATE:

DATE:

DATE:

DATE:

DATE:

DATE:

DATE:

Try to be grateful for the
things that upset and unbalance
you. We can only uncover true
enduring gratitude by learning to be
grateful for every aspect of our lives.
The good. The bad. The ugly. Life is
made of all these things and they are
constantly interacting with each other.
To be grateful for life means being
grateful for everything that
comes with it.

DATE:

START WHERE YOU ARE. USE WHAT YOU HAVE.

DATE:

DATE:

DO WHAT YOU CAN.   ~ ARTHUR ASHE

DATE:

DATE:

DATE:

DATE:

Don't underestimate
the importance of
balance. If you make balance
a principle in your life, you'll find
life so much easier to keep afloat.
This goes in both directions. Try to balance
out all the indulgences in your life so you
don't overdo it. But also, a little bit of
indulgence can be fun and renewing. If you
find yourself indulging, don't start criticising
yourself. Instead, remember that there is an
ebb and flow to all things; if you are mindful
of the thing you are indulging in, over time
it will balance itself out.

DATE:

_____
_____
_____
_____
_____
_____
_____
_____
_____
_____

WE DO NOT REMEMBER DAYS.

DATE:

_____
_____
_____
_____
_____
_____
_____
_____
_____
_____

DATE:

WE REMEMBER MOMENTS. ~ CESARE PAVESE

DATE:

DATE:

DATE:

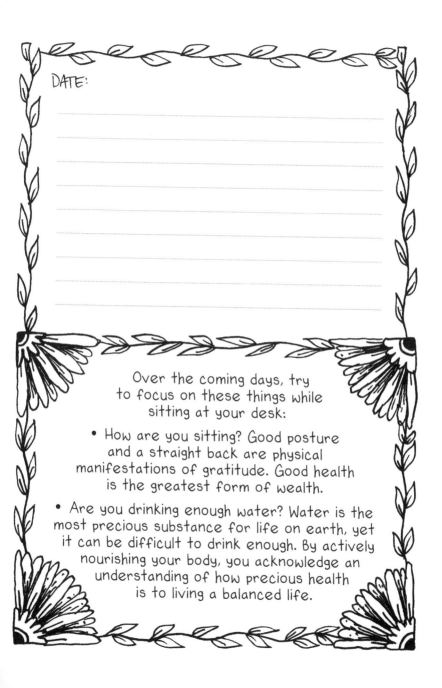

DATE:

Over the coming days, try
to focus on these things while
sitting at your desk:

• How are you sitting? Good posture
and a straight back are physical
manifestations of gratitude. Good health
is the greatest form of wealth.

• Are you drinking enough water? Water is the
most precious substance for life on earth, yet
it can be difficult to drink enough. By actively
nourishing your body, you acknowledge an
understanding of how precious health
is to living a balanced life.

DATE:

ONE OF THE SECRETS OF LIFE IS TO MAKE

DATE:

DATE:

STEPPING STONES OUT OF STUMBLING BLOCKS. ~JACK PENN

DATE:

DATE:

DATE:

DATE:

We often hold on to ideas we think
are true because they are comforting and
convenient. But does convenience mean that
what we consider to be true is actually
good for us and the world? It is worth
looking at the things you hold to be
true and questioning whether these
truths are a source of positive growth or
a way to justify actions that may actually
lead to harm for yourself or others.

THOSE WHO DO NOT KNOW HOW TO WEEP

DATE:

WITH THEIR WHOLE HEART

DATE:

DON'T KNOW HOW TO LAUGH EITHER. - GOLDA MEIR

DATE:

DATE:

DATE:

DATE:

DATE:

....

....

....

....

....

....

....

When we experience something that
causes us to feel gratitude, the sun
coming out from behind a cloud, a cool
breeze on a hot day or hearing the
laughter of someone we love, we can
show we are grateful for the opportunity
by creating opportunities for others to
be grateful. Send an email telling a friend
how much they mean to you, donate
your time to the less fortunate or even
just smile and be friendly to someone
you pass in the street.

DATE:

DATE:

HOPE IS A WAKING DREAM.

DATE:

_____

DATE:

ARISTOTLE

DATE:

DATE:

DATE:

Fear is a waste of the imagination.
When we think about the future,
the choice is with us whether we imagine
a future filled with scenarios where things have
gone wrong or one where our hard work pays
off and our intentions are fulfilled. Save your
imagination for creating fun, exciting things
and try not to waste it on thoughts that
create fear and anxiety.

DATE:

IT IS NOT ENOUGH TO BE COMPASSIONATE,

DATE:

DATE:

WE MUST ACT. ~ DALAI LAMA[xiv]

DATE:

DATE:

DATE:

DATE:

It can be hard to hear and absorb suggestions and criticism about oneself. How we choose to live our lives is deeply personal to each of us. However, I have found that if I can acknowledge all criticisms about myself with openness, not giving in to feelings of anger or ego, I can choose if some are worth implementing into my life in hopes of becoming a better person. Some criticism may be of benefit, even if we find it hard to hear at first.

DATE:

DATE:

DATE:

DATE:

DATE:

DATE:

DATE:

Breathe.

DATE:

DATE:

DATE:

FALL SEVEN TIMES, STAND UP EIGHT. ~ JAPANESE PROVERB

DATE:

DATE:

DATE:

DATE:

Smile.

DATE:

WHEN YOU GO, THE ROAD IS ROUGH;

DATE:

DATE:

WHEN YOU RETURN, SMOOTH. - THAI PROVERB

DATE:

DATE:

DATE:

DATE:

Breathe and smile.

DATE:

THERE IS NO SUCH THING AS FAILURE.

DATE:

DATE:

YOU EITHER SUCCEED OR LEARN. ~ KEVIN KRUSE

DATE:

DATE:

DATE:

DATE:

Over the coming days, try to focus
on these things as you are walking:

• Where do you set your gaze?
Are you looking down at your feet?
Or around you, taking in the sights?

• How steady is your breath?

• Do you move quickly, only walking to get where
you need to be instead of being where you are?

Travelling is a perfect time to practise
walking meditation. Pick a stretch of
your walk and every time you walk
it remember to be mindful of the
world and yourself at that moment.

MARCEL
PROUST

DATE:

DATE:

DATE:

DATE:

DATE:

DATE:

DATE:

_____

_____

_____

_____

_____

_____

_____

_____

_____

Often the things in our lives
that we end up complaining about
are the worst part of the best things.
A good example is friendship. Sometimes
friends can upset or annoy us and this is
the worst part of having friends, while at
the same time having friends can be one of
the most fulfilling experiences in life. The
same idea can be applied to our jobs, our
diets and so many other parts of our lives.

DATE:

DATE:

DISCIPLINE IS THE BRIDGE BETWEEN GOALS AND ACCOMPLISHMENT. ~ JIM ROHN

DATE:

DATE:

DATE:

DATE:

DATE:

Go for a hike on a sunny day
and you will see that living creatures
love the sun. The birds will be soaring high and
chirping loudly. Rabbits, squirrels and deer will
make their appearance, rushing to open spaces
to absorb the warming sun. The first sunny
day after a rainy stretch and I can feel my
heart warming and happiness flooding my mind.
Positivity has the same effect as the sun.
Act with kindness, encouragement
and love, and living creatures will flock
to be warmed by these things.

DATE:

NEVER UNDERESTIMATE THE POWER

DATE:

DATE:

OF PASSION. ~ EVE SAWYER

DATE:

DATE:

DATE:

DATE:

For me, the most important spiritual ideas
are the simplest ones. Act out of love.
Show compassion to all beings. Go easy on
yourself. They are simple to learn but for
some reason take a lifetime to remember,
and so we need to make time to remind
ourselves of them every day.

DATE:

DATE:

THINGS WHICH MATTER MOST MUST NEVER BE AT THE MERCY

DATE:

DATE:

OF THINGS WHICH MATTER LEAST.   ~ GOETHE

DATE:

_____

_____

_____

_____

_____

_____

_____

_____

_____

DATE:

_____

_____

_____

_____

_____

_____

_____

_____

_____

DATE:

Begin your day with gratitude before you get out of bed. Even if the schedule for the day ahead is filled with tasks you are nervous about, take some time to acknowledge what is good about the moment you are in:

• The access you have to clean water which enables you to take a shower and brush your teeth and feel more awake to start your day.

• The security of the room you're in and how it allows you to have a moment of reflection.

Begin your day with gratitude and positive thinking and it will create a hue and tone that colours the rest of your day.

I'M GOING HOME LIKE A SHOOTING STAR.

SOJOURNER TRUTH

DATE:

SOME RUN SWIFTLY; SOME CREEP PAINFULLY;

DATE:

DATE:

ALL WHO KEEP ON WILL REACH THE GOAL. ~ PIYADASSI THERA

DATE:

DATE:

DATE:

DATE:

When starting to write this book,
I had to learn how to see the lessons
around me and then write them down.
But before long I realised that there
is a lesson in just about everything.
Inanimate objects. Living creatures.
Pretty much anything in nature. Every
observable object has a lesson to teach
us but only if we have the eyes to see
it and openness to learn it.

DATE:

IF YOUR COMPASSION DOES NOT INCLUDE YOURSELF,

DATE:

DATE:

IT IS INCOMPLETE.   ~   JACK KORNFIELD

DATE:

DATE:

DATE:

DATE:

Taking time to reflect on the
current season reconnects us
with the rhythms of the natural world.
Winter reminds us of the importance of
introspection and rest. Winter prepares us
for Spring, when we can grow and reach
out towards the light that life offers.
We are all travelling together through
the cycles of the seasons.

DATE:

IT IS NOT THE   PERFECT BUT THE   IMPERFECT

DATE:

DATE:

WHO HAVE NEED OF LOVE. ~ OSCAR WILDE

DATE:

DATE:

DATE:

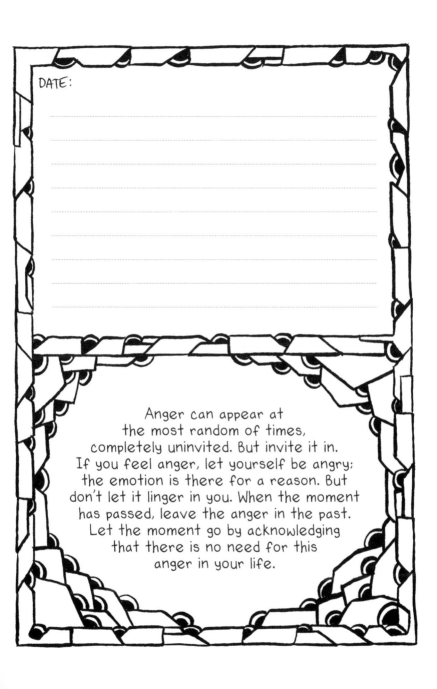

DATE:

Anger can appear at
the most random of times,
completely uninvited. But invite it in.
If you feel anger, let yourself be angry;
the emotion is there for a reason. But
don't let it linger in you. When the moment
has passed, leave the anger in the past.
Let the moment go by acknowledging
that there is no need for this
anger in your life.

DATE:

DATE:

THE HIGHEST FORM OF THOUGHT; AND THAT GRATITUDE

DATE:

_____
_____
_____
_____
_____
_____
_____
_____
_____

DATE:

_____
_____
_____
_____
_____
_____
_____
_____
_____

IS HAPPINESS DOUBLED BY WONDER. ~ G.K. CHESTERTON

DATE:

DATE:

DATE:

_____
_____
_____
_____
_____
_____
_____

It is important to remember
that there is no moment but this
moment. If at this moment you are
acting out of love, then your whole world is
love. If you are acting out of hate, then use
this moment to address that. Take life one
moment at a time, trying your best to be
a well of positivity. We cannot change the
past or control the future, but at
this moment we can choose to
be a source of light.

DATE:

DATE:

THE BEST THINGS IN LIFE ARE YOURS IF

YOU CAN APPRECIATE YOURSELF. ~ DALE CARNEGIE

DATE:

DATE:

DATE:

DATE:

DATE:

Try to build
activities into your
day that are also reminders
of important lessons. If you have
a daily task that requires patience to
be completed properly, like dusting the
house or collecting firewood, use this as
a chance to remember the importance
of patience in life and also as a daily
opportunity to improve your
ability to be patient.

DATE:

DATE:

ALL GREAT ACHIEVEMENTS REQUIRE TIME. ~ MAYA ANGELOU

DATE:

DATE:

DATE:

DATE:

DATE:

Let go of the things
holding you back. Breathe
deeply and be here in this
moment. Reach out for the future
with passion and focus. Live
the life you want to live.

DATE:

ALWAYS BE A FIRST RATE VERSION OF YOURSELF INSTEAD

DATE:

DATE:

OF A SECOND RATE VERSION OF SOMEONE ELSE. JUDY GARLAND

DATE:

DATE:

DATE:

DATE:

We can show gratitude for our
life by living it, by using the time
we are given to experience as
much of life as possible.

DATE:

YOU CANNOT TREAD THE PATH

DATE:

DATE:

BEFORE YOU BECOME THE PATH YOURSELF. - ZEN SAYING

DATE:

DATE:

DATE:

DATE:

Our daily lives are often
full of extraordinary events,
but they can become commonplace
as we experience them day after
day. If you were living in a place with
a lack of clean water, then having a
sink with a faucet that gushes fresh
cool water would be so much
more amazing to you.

DATE:

DATE:

DREAMS COME TRUE; WITHOUT THAT POSSIBILITY,

DATE:

DATE:

NATURE WOULD NOT INCITE US TO HAVE THEM. ~ JOHN UPDIKE

DATE:

DATE:

DATE:

To be grateful for life,
we must first learn how
to be grateful for death.
Truly acknowledging our
impermanence is the first step
towards appreciating the limited
time we have to be alive.

DATE:

SEEK NOT TO FOLLOW IN THE FOOTSTEPS OF THE WISE;

DATE:

DATE:

SEEK WHAT THEY SOUGHT. ~ MATSUO BASHŌ

DATE:

DATE:

DATE:

DATE:

_____

_____

_____

_____

_____

_____

_____

_____

Try not to dwell too much on your
own mortality. Yes, you will die. But today
you are alive and that is what matters.
If we spend too much time worrying
about death, we are only wasting the time
we do have. You have all eternity to be
dead, so be alive while you still are.

DATE:

EVERYTHING HAS BEAUTY.

DATE:

DATE:

BUT NOT EVERYONE CAN SEE IT. — CONFUCIUS

DATE:

DATE:

DATE:

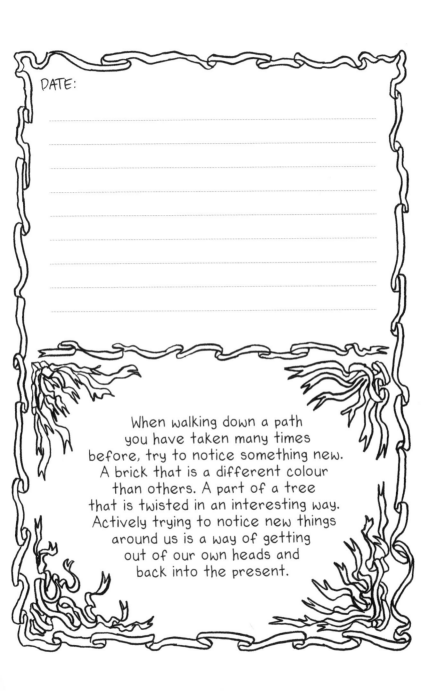

DATE:

When walking down a path
you have taken many times
before, try to notice something new.
A brick that is a different colour
than others. A part of a tree
that is twisted in an interesting way.
Actively trying to notice new things
around us is a way of getting
out of our own heads and
back into the present.

DATE:

WHAT YOU DO HAS FAR GREATER IMPACT

DATE:

DATE:

THAN WHAT YOU SAY. ~ STEPHEN COVEY

DATE:

DATE:

DATE:

DATE:

Over the coming days, try to build time
into your schedule to not be staring at a
screen. Choose activities that are tactile
and non-digital. Pull out a deck of cards or
a puzzle and tangibly engage your senses.

GRATITUDE
IS THE
MEMORY

OF THE

HEART.

JEAN BAPTISTE MASSIEU

DATE:

IF I HAD TO LIVE MY LIFE AGAIN, I'D MAKE

DATE:

DATE:

THE SAME MISTAKES, ONLY SOONER. ~ TALLULAH BANKHEAD

DATE:

DATE:

DATE:

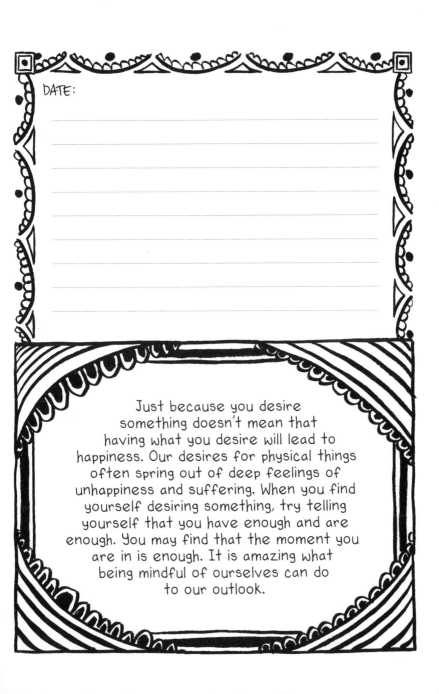

DATE:

Just because you desire
something doesn't mean that
having what you desire will lead to
happiness. Our desires for physical things
often spring out of deep feelings of
unhappiness and suffering. When you find
yourself desiring something, try telling
yourself that you have enough and are
enough. You may find that the moment you
are in is enough. It is amazing what
being mindful of ourselves can do
to our outlook.

DATE:

DATE:

IN THE MIDDLE OF DIFFICULTY LIES OPPORTUNITY. ~ ALBERT EINSTEIN

DATE:

_____
_____
_____
_____
_____
_____
_____
_____
_____
_____

DATE:

_____
_____
_____
_____
_____
_____
_____
_____
_____
_____

DATE:

DATE:

DATE:

Today will never come again.
Will it be a good day? Or a bad day?
A day filled with love or with friction?
Each day is a gift and you can show
gratitude for it by making it a day
to remember for yourself and
the people around you.

NOTES, QUOTES
AND ANYTHING ELSE

TO TRAVEL HOPEFULLY IS A BETTER THING THAN TO ARRIVE.

ROBERT LOUIS STEVENSON